Podcast Strategies:
21 Questions Answered

http://www.PodcastStrategiesBook.com

Paul Colligan
with Mike Koenigs and Gene Naftulyev

Podcast Strategies: 21 Questions Answered

Special Offer / Register This Book

The world of Podcasting is changing all the time. We want to make sure you are kept up to date with the latest information.

Register this book so that we can keep you up to date with all things Podcasting. In addition, we'd like to send you the following items, that couldn't, for obvious reasons, be included in this book:

- Immediate delivery of a **90 minute HD video** the covers many of the Podcasting topics and questions covered in this book. You'll be able to stream the video, or download it for viewing on the device of your choice.

- Access to our constantly updated **Online Podcast Gear Guide**. Included inside is direct links to the perfect products at the best prices we could find online. Access to this document could save you thousands of dollars alone.

- Download access to **10 royalty-free music tracks** that you can use in your Podcasts.

- An online list (with links) of **our favorite Podcasts** (always changing).

- A few more bonuses that we want to surprise you with.

To get your bonuses, send a copy of your receipt to:

Bonuses@PodcastStrategiesBook.com

… and we'll do the rest.

Table Of Contents

Podcast?

About The Authors

PAUL COLLIGAN helps others leverage technology to improve themselves and broaden their audience with reduced stress and no drama. He does this with a lifestyle and business designed to answer the challenges and opportunities of this new economy. If you are looking for titles: Husband, Father, YouTube Expert, Bestselling Author, Director of Content Marketing for InstantCustomer.com and CEO of Colligan.com. He lives in Portland, Oregon.

Also By Paul Colligan:

- YouTube Strategies: Making And Marketing Online Video
- Cross Channel Social Media Marketing

MIKE KOENIGS is a two-time #1 Bestselling Author, "2009 Marketer of the Year", entrepreneur, filmmaker, speaker and holds a patent in "Cross-Channel" Marketing Technology. He is the CEO, "Chief Disruptasaurus" and Founder of Traffic Geyser and Instant Customer. His products simplify marketing for tens of thousands of small businesses, authors, experts, speakers, coaches and consultants in over 60 countries. His celebrity and bestselling author clients and friends include Paula Abdul, Tony Robbins, Tim Ferriss, Debbie Ford, John

Assaraf from "The Secret", Brian Tracy, Jorge Cruise, Dan Kennedy and Harvey MacKay.

Also By Mike Koenigs:

- Author Expert Marketing Machines: The Ultimate 5-Step, Push-Button, Automated System to Become the Expert, Authority and Star in Your Niche
- Make Market Launch IT: The Ultimate Product Creation System for Turning Your Ideas Into Income

GENE NAFTULYEV is a C-Level executive, author, speaker, business consultant, and auditor with a proven record of successfully building and managing organizations over the last 20 years. His experience starting, owning and operating small businesses along with auditing very large firms gives him the ability to bring a wealth of knowledge to the table. In his spare time he is a fine art photographer with over 20 years behind the lens and an avid technologist who has hosted several Podcasts since 2007.

About This Book

Imagine this: your media / your content automatically delivered to the smartphone, television and iPod (or iPad) of your audience, with no one standing between you and them.

You've got a show and it arrives, automatically, every time you release something new. You are "the Media."

The Internet just got bigger.

Forget Google. Your content can be delivered to Apple iPhones, streamed to Visio Blu-ray players, viewed on Sony televisions and listened to on BMW car stereos. Your audience can now consume your content when and where they want: at the gym, on their daily commute, on an international flight and on their living room couch.

Podcasting makes it all possible — and I know your message is worth Podcasting.

My history with Podcasting is a long one. Once the tech (invented by Adam Curry and Dave Winer) made possible the syndicated distribution of media over the Internet — I've never looked back. I don't believe you will either

(especially by the time you are done with this book.)

When my audience automatically receives my content (at the time and place of their choosing), everything changes. Podcasting has helped me get my message out *to more people* than I ever could have imagined, *with less effort* than I could have dreamed, for *more profit* than anyone would have guessed.

It's been a wild ride.

I love Podcasting and it is a big part of my business. I have published hundreds of episodes (for myself and others), taught a half-dozen courses to hundreds of students, and published another book on the topic before anyone knew what an iPhone was.

So, about this book ...

Over the years, I get asked many of the same questions over and over. Questions such as ...

- What is a Podcast? Is Podcasting audio only?
- Why is Podcasting the "next big thing" again? What has changed?
- Why should I Podcast?
- What equipment and/or software do I need to make a Podcast?
- How do I make money from my Podcast?
- And more ...

In this book I answer those questions and 16 others. It was designed to be a fast read with no fluff.

You deserve better than that. You are ready to get to work and the answer to these questions is obviously step #1.

When done you should be able to take this information and plot your own Podcast Strategies (hence the title).

This book is part of a larger project for Traffic Geyser and Instant Customer, of which I am their Director of Content. They have a few tools, right now that can be used in Podcasting – and a few surprises coming in the future – but nothing written in this book requires either. I do recommend them though.

I'm sure there are typos in this book and that we missed a few things. Do us both a favor and register this book (directions are a few pages back) so we can keep you up to date when we change things.

Paul Colligan
Portland, Oregon
Podcast Strategies 1.0
May 2013

QUESTION ONE

What is a Podcast? Is Podcasting audio only?

"Looks can be deceiving"...we've all heard it. Similarly, words can be deceiving too! Although the term *Podcast* borrows its name from the popular Apple digital audio player, you don't have to own an iPod to create or listen to one. As Wikipedia explains, a Podcast is "a type of digital media consisting of an episodic series of audio, video, PDF, or ePub files subscribed to and downloaded through Web syndication or streamed online."

Cutting through all that wordiness, a Podcast can be better described as "episodic, digital media available online via subscription or on-demand." At its core, it's just a GREAT way to deliver content!

By far, the biggest benefit of Podcasting is the easy consumption of content. Instead of being tethered to a computer, people can now listen to Podcasts in the car, on the airplane, on their television, while they are at the gym - on a bike or treadmill.

I have literally seen people lifting weights looking down at, or listening to, their phones. One doesn't have to drive far to see the car next to them paying more attention to a device than the road. Podcasting moves your content from being isolated to the web browser to media when you want it, where you want it, and how you want it.

The '800-pound gorilla' in the room is audio—(at the time of writing) 20 percent of all drivers are already listening to online audio, making it something you really want to be part of. It's a form of rapid content creation and distribution that can be extremely profitable when done correctly.

But, remember, the car isn't the only place one consumes Podcasts.

Check out these statistics: According to Pugh Research, the growth of people listening to online radio in their cars via a cell phone—just that alone—has grown almost 100 percent per year. Right now, about 11 percent of the population of the U.S. listens to audio on their mobile phones. Also, the percentage of consumers indicating that they are listening to audio Podcasts has grown 163 percent from 11 percent in 2006, to 29 percent in 2012.

It's mind-blowing!

To top it off, Podcasting is not only limited to audio. As briefly mentioned before, it can also be delivered via video, PDF files, ePub files or any other digital media made available episodically or via subscription.

Have you ever fantasized about having your content distributed amid the likes of Rachel Maddow, the NBC Nightly News, or National Public Radio (NPR)? Well, Podcasting provides this opportunity.

The beauty of Podcasting is that it literally takes minutes to create and publish a Podcast. You can learn how to do it in under an hour and it can be published on iTunes for free. It literally takes about three to five minutes to submit your Podcast, after which it's generally approved and available to subscribe to and download within 24 hours. Once it's published, your Podcast is available to the entire world at the mere click of a button.

And, did I mention, this process doesn't cost you a dime?

It's not just an issue of on-demand media. Podcasts also allow subscription – a means to automatically receive every new episode of a show you've subscribed to, automatically, as soon as it is available.

Am I saying that a Podcast subscribed to early one year brings continuous content for years to come? Yes. Again, this is why we love the technology so much.

And contrary to its misleading name, Podcasting can be consumed—from creation, to distribution, to subscribing and accessing—on many different devices. In addition to the iPhone, iPad or iPod, it's assessable on the Android phone, Windows 8 phone, Apple TV, Google TV and even your Sony Blu-ray player, to name a few.

It is a remarkable mechanism to give away (and deliver) content, to attract people to you, and to build relationships which give you the ability to sell something to them later on. Yes, there are people who currently Podcast who are generating seven figures in revenue a year, just through their Podcasts, with an uncomplicated business model on the back end.

Can we promise that this type of success is a regular occurrence? No, we cannot. However, it is a perfect medium that has finally reached the tipping point, a critical mass, where everything—the devices, hardware, bandwidth and technology to create and distribute it—is here and it's FREE.

Summary

Simply put, a Podcast is any "episodic, digital media available online via subscription or on-demand." This includes audio, video, PDF files, ePub files, or any other digital media made available episodically or via subscription. Audio is the biggest player in this very big game.

The biggest benefits to Podcasting are that it provides an effective means to get and consume content and it's available however, whenever, wherever you want.

Contrary to its misleading name, you don't have to own an iPod in order to create or listen to a Podcast. Podcasts can be accessed on numerous devices such as smart phones, tablets, televisions, Blu-ray players, and across multiple operating systems.

It's a form of rapid content creation and distribution that practically anyone in the world can use. It's everywhere and if done intelligently and strategically, it's also highly profitable!

Action Items

1. Make Podcasting your go-to source for rapidly getting your content out.

2. Although audio Podcasting is the 800-pound gorilla, consider using it to also deliver video, PDF files, ePub files or any other digital media you want to make available episodically or via subscription.

3. Use Podcasts to build relationships, strengthening your rapport and ability to sell products and services to your audience at a later date.

QUESTION TWO

Why is Podcasting the next big thing? What has changed?

Wait a minute, wasn't Podcasting "the next big thing" 7 years ago?

On the Internet, exciting, popular and sexy trends come...and just as quickly, they go. When *The Business Podcasting Bible* was written in 2006, the iPhone wasn't even a rumor! Remarkably, Podcasting was sexy then and it's sexy now. Heck, it's sexier ...

So, what's changed? Why am I covering the topic again?

First, and this is important, the numbers in support of Podcasting never went down. To the contrary, they've been going up since 2006. No matter which way you look at it or how you track it, the numbers have been consistently going up. More and more people are consuming Podcasts than the year before. More and more Podcasts are being consumed than the year before.

Initially the concept was primarily contained within the Podcast enthusiast and tech communities. Although it experienced a meteoric rise (often in hype alone), it eventually peaked because the original Podcasting process required too many steps and was too geeky for many. Another fact, that we mentioned previously, is that the term "Podcasting" might have gotten in the way as well. To this day, many people still think they can't listen to Podcasts because they don't have an iPod.

But something quite remarkable happened that changed the way people could access Podcasts. The Smart Phone with cheap/fast Internet connectivity happened. I'm not just talking the iPhone here–this is an issue of Android, Blackberry and Microsoft phones—even companies you've never heard of. People now had the ability to listen to on-demand, episodic content, however they want, whenever they want, with a phone connected to the Internet.

On demand media has always been possible through YouTube and the Web, but not everyone's in front of the computer day and night. However, people have their phones by their side 24x7, carrying them in their pockets and purses, connecting in their cars the second they get in via Bluetooth. Now, high speed connectivity allows us to access Podcasts in the instant we want them without having to worry about going through the process of logging into our computers and syncing our phones.

Quite simply, we've hit critical mass because technology has made it easier.

And that same technology is probably in your pocket right now.

Is that a smile on your face?

The marketplace has also matured considerably. Psychological barriers are coming down as people are getting used to obtaining their content over the Internet through online service providers like Netflix, Hulu, or Amazon's Kindle. They're used to seeing content as a profitable, viable thing that doesn't have to come from ABC, CBS or NBC anymore.

Amazon deserves a lot of credit in this arena. With such a massive percentage of all books being distributed by them, the publishing industry is being decimated and people are used to no longer looking to "traditional" providers for their media content. Amazon is selling up to three times as many books through the Kindle platform as the regular printed edition. Heck, you're probably reading this book on a Kindle right now smiling. The idea of physical ownership of content is no longer important to many audiences that once thought, not too long ago, that the iPod was "for the kids."

The content is important—as it should be—and the Internet is how we're getting it.

As a niche provider, you can be an expert in your field and yet it's unlikely that mainstream media will pick you up. When Podcasting was first sexy, there was a good chance that your audience didn't know what a Podcast was and certainly wasn't looking to the Internet to deliver their media.

So much has changed. Traditional broadcast media, whether it is television or radio, is simply not a practical means to get your content out. For example, you might be a nutritionist who wants to create your own radio or television show. Although it's unlikely you'll get on T.V., you could start your own television-quality show for almost no money and be up and broadcasting in under a day. At some point, after you've developed an audience, you could eventually transition into mainstream media.

A great example of a successful niche provider is TED (which stands for Technology, Entertainment, Design.) TED is a nonprofit devoted to *Ideas Worth Spreading* and has established an award-winning TED Talks video site. All you have to do is subscribe to TED Talks on your preferred device and every time a new video comes out, it is automatically downloaded and ready for listening. It is one of my favorite Podcasts. No, more than that, it is one of my favorite sources of content anywhere. It simply wasn't possible when my first book came out.

Let's face it. With the rise of on-demand programming broadcast television is losing its hold. Right now, Netflix is logging more content views in certain programs than broadcast and Direct TV combined. It just goes to show that the convenience factor is going to win. Now that technology has caught up with convenience, Podcasting is practical, reasonable and realistic for everyone. Internet-connected phones have made it as easy to get Podcast content as changing the dial on the radio.

Bottom-line, Podcasting has always been around; it has always been growing. However, in its current growth pattern, the mainstream market is now coming to it and it is easier to consume than ever before. Getting content from the Internet is extremely exciting and viable, and it is done very, very well. The time to get on board is now. If you want to grab onto something that has a huge upside potential, Podcasting is it.

Now more than ever …

Summary

Why is Podcasting the next big thing? Truth is, it's always been big! The numbers have been going up since 2006 and they haven't stopped.

Technology is no longer getting in the way and the psychological barrier of getting content from the Internet is evaporating. Internet connected phones are making access ridiculously easy and at a very low price.

New service providers like Amazon, Netflix and Hulu are decimating mainstream media and publishing, as we know it. You can be part of that trend.

Now that technology has met up with the convenience factor, Podcasting is practical, realistic and profitable. Podcasting is still on the rise and you want to be part of it.

Action Items

1. Use Podcasting as a means to get beyond mainstream and establish yourself as an expert in your field and connect with your audience.

2. Take advantage of the fact that technologic and psychological barriers are lifting, making Podcasting not only viable, but also profitable.

3. Podcasting has reached critical mass, the time for Podcasting is now and it's only getting stronger. Step up and be part of it.

QUESTION THREE

Why should I Podcast?

It's not unusual for people to invest in equipment and technology and then ask, "Okay, I have my high definition video camera. What should I Podcast about?" We call it the *fire-aim-ready syndrome*. Instead of ready-aim-fire, they tend to produce and then wonder why nobody is listening. Don't do this. Do not fire-aim-ready. It should be *ready-aim-fire*.

There are really only three reasons to Podcast. We call these the **three P's of Podcasting**.

First, if you are **passionate** about a topic and you want to get the word out about it, Podcasting is a great platform. We love passion and we are passionate about Podcasting.

However, we do not subscribe to the Kevin Costner School of Business. This is not a situation where "if you build it, they will come." Passion isn't always enough. To this day I have to deal with the implications of a famous Podcaster who once said "Podcast your Passion and the Profits will follow." There are a few points missing from that statement.

Passion is beautiful; passion is wonderful, but it is not necessarily enough. Passion with profit, however, is very, very doable – if you plan accordingly.

The second reason to Podcast is **position**. You can position yourself incredibly well with a Podcast. One of the earliest people in the Podcasting industry, *Grammar Girl*, received a book contract because of her Podcast. The best part is that she was asked to be on Oprah's Winfrey's talk show because of her Podcast, *before she even had the book done*! However, once she knew she was going to be on Oprah and had nothing to pitch; she took all of the past episodes of her Podcast, created an audio book from it and uploaded it to iTunes. Even with no mention of a book, or anything to buy, Grammar Girl created an audio book that remained a top-seller in iTunes for several months after her appearance.

Thanks to this technology, you don't have to wait to publish your content anymore. If you have a great idea, you can talk about it, click the publish button, and bam! It is available worldwide to stream and download to any device imaginable, with no distribution challenges.

Let's face it. Virtually every business challenge really comes down to a marketing or distribution problem. Podcasting addresses both of those. It is a great way to start a conversation and create engagement with your listeners and viewers, spurring them on to investigate your products or services further. Ultimately, if done effectively, they will end up buying your books, audio programs and services.

A great example of this is Kevin Rose and *Diggnation*. Kevin had a program that was essentially one of the biggest Podcasts on Revision3, one of the leading independent free online video services. Kevin, along with his co-founder, Alex, was able to position himself as a technology and start up expert—and bam!—he became a top dog over at Google working as a venture partner. He would not have been given that opportunity without making himself very, very visible. Again, the Podcast was his positioning device.

By the way, the Discover Channel recently purchased Revision3 for a rumored 30 million dollars. Nice, eh? Passion with a plan can do some amazing things.

Like *Grammar Girl* and *Diggnation*, you too can position yourself as the go-to person in your industry or niche through Podcasting!

Lastly, the third P word, our favorite, is **profit**. If you go in with a strategy and a system for profiting from your Podcasting, amazing things can happen. We are all for passion; we are all for positioning; however, throwing in a little strategy and going in with a *profit game*, will lead to your greatest success.

Summary

Why should you Podcast? The classic approach is to jump into the technical aspect of Podcasting, only secondarily thinking about the 'what' and 'why' of Podcasting. This is called the fire-aim-ready approach. In order to be successful, you need to focus on and execute *ready-aim-fire*.

There are only three reasons to Podcast. They are what we call the three P's to Podcasting: *passion*, *positioning* and *profit*. Develop a strategy and figure out what elements of passion, position, and profit are parts of your plan and amazing results are within your reach.

Action Items

1. Identify which aspects of the three P's of Podcasting—passion, position and profit—apply to you and set about strategically implementing them.

2. **Passion**. Determine what you are passionate about and use Podcasting as a platform to push your content out to your audience.

3. **Position** yourself as the go-to person within your field of expertise using your Podcast.

4. **Profit**. Develop a strategy and system to profit from your Podcasting.

QUESTION FOUR

What equipment and/or software do I need to make a Podcast?

What about equipment? Well, let's dig into the details....

Microphone

First, you need a microphone for recording audio. The great thing is that the one attached to your phone might just be good enough. Alternatively, there are dozens of USB microphones that you can buy for a reasonable price on Amazon.com. This doesn't have to be a fancy; you just need a basic microphone to record audio.

You will always want to sound as good as possible and present the highest quality Podcast that you can. The old commercial was right when it told you that you "never have a second chance to make a first impression."

Ultimately, however, your content is more important than the quality of your Podcast. There is a Podcast episode of the *I Love Marketing* that illustrates this point well. During the episode they interviewed a celebrity over the phone. The entire recording is a rather low quality recording of a phone conversation between the two hosts and a major celebrity. However, low recording quality aside, it generated over a quarter of a million downloads – and is regarded by their audience as one of their best shows ever!

So, don't worry about the actual microphone itself. Get the highest quality you can, but don't let your focus on "quality" stop you from Podcasting. It is all about the content. Start out by experimenting with what you have and see if you're happy with the results.

Video Camera

What about video? If you decide to make video part of your Podcasting mix, you'll probably need a video camera. Chances are that you already have one to use— your smart phone! The video camera and microphone on Smart Phones these days actually work remarkably well. If not, there are dozens of affordable, high-definition video options available on Amazon.com. We are big fans of the Kodak Z series—the Zi8, Zi9 and Zi10. They are all wonderful options and are all currently available for under a hundred dollars now that Kodak has left the video camera game.

Probably need a video camera? The immensely popular and profitable "Screencasts Online" Podcast went years recording only Don McAllister's Mac Desktop before he never put his face on video.

This might be surprising, but great audio with mediocre video does much better than great video with mediocre audio. Plan your Podcast Strategies accordingly!

Just because you can, doesn't mean you should. An audio Podcast can reach many more people than a video Podcast because there are many more places where an audio Podcast can be consumed.

Do the math and plan accordingly before you invest in a video camera.

Text Production

If you are Podcasting text in an eBook or PDF format, the only equipment you'll need is your computer and whatever word processing software you prefer.

Many, including us, have switched to Google Docs / Google Drive for the (free) online collaboration and hosting of content. All of the tools within can export as PDF files. The most popular format for text-based Podcasting.

Editing Software

Don't fool yourself; you're not going to get your content perfect on the first take. You will need audio and/or video editing software. Our favorite audio editing and recording software is Audacity. Audacity is great because it works on all operating systems—Mac, PC or Linux—and it's absolutely FREE. If you own a Mac, you have the ability to use GarageBand that comes as standard audio editing software when you buy the computer. If you are on a PC and you want something a little more complicated, you can get the Sony Sound Forge editor. This software is currently under a hundred dollars as well.

The first rule of editing software is "go with what you know." If you are familiar with one specific platform, there is no need to learn another one, at least initially, to create and manage your Podcast.

For video editing, iMovie is the free, standard software that comes with every Mac computer. Sony Movie Studio (formally Sony Vegas) works great on the PC for video editing.

Additional Requirements

Once you create, record, and save your Podcast content you have to put it online in order to distribute it in a downloadable format. You'll need some sort of online media host. You'll also need what is known as an "RSS Feed" to make your Podcast content information available to all of the providers – iTunes and the like.

First of all, don't let this part of the process intimidate

you. There are systems out there that do everything for you. In this day and age, if you are attempting to do anything a computer should be doing, well, that's just the makings of bad science-fiction movie!

Both your media host and your RSS provider need to be Podcast compliant. If they're not compliant, Apple will let you know when you try to submit your Podcast – so trying to go with a host that doesn't support the process will only end up wasting your time.

If you have surfed around the Internet for any amount of time, you've probably seen many Web hosting platforms that advertise unlimited bandwidth. Most of them do for HTML and graphics; however, not all do it for Podcasting because many people abuse it.

If you don't know, simply ask the service provider, "Can I support/serve Podcasts on this host, yes or no?" They are easy to find, so search Google accordingly.

One last word to the wise—find a Podcasting host that doesn't go down!

Side note: Since I work there, I have to point out, Traffic Geyser has a tool that will both host your content and provide the RSS feed. FWIW, the entire Season One of eMarketingVids was produced using Traffic Geyser and we'll be doing the same with Season 2 (coming out very soon). You can head over to Traffic Geyser, take look at it and take advantage of the one-dollar trial if you so wish. They are by no means the only one. Google should lead you to great lists and our Podcast Gear And Services Guide, which is yours free when you register this book. It will give you a list of plenty of other choices.

Summary

What equipment do you need? You need a microphone, if you are just recording audio; a video camera for video Podcasting; and a word processor/computer of your choice is to manage text.

Audio editing is cheap and/or free. Video editing is cheap and/or free. Word processing is cheap and/or free. You can do all of these on your computer.

Service-wise, you will need somebody to create your RSS feed in a Podcast-compliant format and obtain a hosting platform that supports your Podcasting. Remember, not all of them do. Find one that does. It should be simple and easy.

Action Items

1. Buy a microphone if you are recording audio. Nothing fancy, just a basic microphone to get started. There are many great options around or below one hundred dollars available on Amazon. Register your copy of this book (send a copy of

your   receipt   to
Bonuses@PodcastStrategiesBook.com)   to   get
access to our online equipment guide, which will
let you know all of the options we recommend.

2. If you are hoping to video Podcast, and you don't
   already have a video camera capability on your
   smart phone (or aren't satisfied with it), buy an
   inexpensive video camera. There are dozens of
   affordable options available on Amazon. Again
   refer to our online guide for more information.

3. Use a computer, tablet or other word processor to
   manage your text-based content. Don't forget that
   Google Drive is a remarkable tool to collaborate
   and edit, share, and create files for Podcasting.

4. Obtain audio or video editing software as needed.
   Most of this is free or very affordable. Our favorite
   audio editing software for both Macs and PCs is
   Audacity.

5. Create your Podcast RSS feed in a Podcast-
   compliant format and obtain a hosting platform
   that supports Podcasting. Again, make sure to
   verify that the host supports Podcasts—simply ask!

6. Want to use a tool that does all of this for you?
   Check out Traffic Geyser's Podcast building tool.

QUESTION FIVE

How do I make money with a Podcast?

Everybody always wants to know how you make money from Podcasting. That's an absolutely fair question. People should be able to make money with their Podcast if they want. The passion often only lasts so long!

Believe it or not, there are three ways to make money from Podcasting.

The first is the **indirect method**. The indirect method is when your profits indirectly arose "because of your content." *Grammar Girl* is a great example of this. She was given a book contract and an appearance on *Oprah* as a result of her Podcast. Other variations of the indirect method include a speaking or consulting gig that comes from someone having listened to your show.

The indirect method is great work if you can get it – but it is a lousy plan. One of my rules in life is: *If somebody offers you money, take it.* However, the fact of the matter is that the indirect method is just not strategic enough to move forward on alone. It's a nice thought, but it's quite unpredictable.

The second way to make money from your Podcast is the **direct method.** This method is based on making money from your Podcast. There is a *good*, *better* and *best* approach to this. Let's talk about all three.

The *Good* approach would be **ads**. You can place ads in your Podcast, however, you need to realize that the ad game is a numbers game and you have to get huge, massive numbers to see any real money.

The *Better* approach is using **commissioned ads**. This is where Podcasting begins to become very powerful. When you have a niche audience specifically interested in what you have to offer, the chance that they might spend money with you because you have something for them is extremely high. It is a very doable and conceivable approach.

Commissioned ads are sometimes called affiliate marketing or online commissioned sales. Whatever you want to call it, commissioned ads (i.e., sponsored stuff) will get you a higher return. With the right audience you can make upwards of 85 times as much as the average Podcast through commissioned sales.

Another option in *Better* is **sponsorships**. A sponsorship model means that, unlike the other options, you are getting paid per viewer with ads. With a commission, you are getting paid when someone buys something when they listen. Sponsorship means that a company or an organization will potentially say, "We will give you $X to be your lead sponsor." In doing this, the company is buying visibility and access to your audience. Sponsorship partnerships can have massive or micro brand potential. Think about it. If you have an audience that is the same audience for a specific niche product, why wouldn't they want to sponsor your show?

The *Best* approach, the one we love, is your own product. Here you use your Podcast to sell your own product. This works tremendously well. Once people take you for a walk on the beach, on their commute, or to the gym and they listen to five, ten, or 15 episodes, they are then ready for what you have to offer next. Selling your own product is a tremendous opportunity.

The third way to make money through your Podcast is the **integrated method.** This is when you make your Podcast part of an integrated strategy. This is a key approach since Podcasting becomes part of your process of multiple touches.

You want to let people know, "I have an email news letter; I have a Webcast; I have physical products; I have virtual products." When Podcasting becomes part of that, you are in a very good position. The bigger you are, or appear to be, the bigger impact you can have.

What is the secret to this? How is an integrated approach to marketing bigger than a Podcast? Do not make your Podcast content available only via Podcast. Instead make it available as many ways as is possible – maybe a live event, a YouTube video, a blog post or anything else you can think of. Since one of the strongest benefits of Podcasting is that your audience can consume your content when, and where, and how they want – provide your content distribution accordingly.

Funny thing is, your blog post or YouTube Video might introduce someone to the Podcast that they didn't know existed.

A good example of this approach is from *I Love Marketing*. Our good friends Joe Polish and Dean Jackson also make their Podcast available through an iPad Magazine. Comedian Marc Maron has a Kindle Fire app that distributes his Podcast content and it is doing tremendously well.

It's important to think of this from a big point of view. Podcasting isn't an end – it's a multi-faceted broadcasting platform that can instantaneously distribute your content to any location, to any device, anywhere in the world. It's one of the most effective ways to build an extremely deep relationship with your target audience.

There is one other side benefit to Podcasting (regardless of what method you use)—SEO. Google loves Podcasts because they take a little more work than a Web page does. If you have a Podcast and you are providing consistent and constant traffic, Google will notice this and you might get a second listing inside of Google as a result of your Podcast.

Summary

There are three ways to make money from Podcasting. Method number one is **indirect** – business or opportunity comes as a result of your Podcast. It is good work if you can get it, but it is not predictable. You cannot build a business plan or a business around it.

Method number two is **direct**. This method is based on making money from your Podcast. There is a *good*, *better*, and *best* approach to this. Ads are "good"; commissioned ads or sponsorships are "better"; and selling your own product is "best."

Method number three is **integrated.** Here you make your Podcast part of an integrated, multi-touch strategy.

Action Items

1. Determine whether you are going to use the indirect, direct, or integrated method to making money with your Podcast.

2. If you go with the direct method, consider the

"best" approach of using your Podcast to sell your own product. If you don't have one, make one.

3. If you decide on using an integrated method, make your Podcast part of your integrated sales strategy, where your process allows for, and provides, multiple content touches.

4. Remember, another side benefit of Podcasting is increased reach for SEO purposes.

QUESTION SIX

What are the steps to making and publishing a Podcast?

There are three steps to making and publishing a Podcast: 1) creating a media file, 2) uploading the media file to the Internet and 3) updating the RSS feed. It's as simple as that!

The first step is to create a media file. This can be an audio, video or a text file. Here, just apply what you know and what's easiest. If you know how to create media using specific a platform, use it. The simpler it is, the better. You want to focus on content, not on creation of the media file.

The default for Podcast audio files is .mp3. The default for video is .mp4. For text, most use .pdf. You can use other file formats if you want, but you can't be assured that all media players can support the format.

You can always have someone else edit the media file for you. There are numerous people out there who can edit your audio, video or text-based content for you. You will be surprised how inexpensive it is.

As we talked about earlier, after you create and upload it, you will need a hosting site that lets you post and stream Podcasts.

Also, make sure you are with a host that does not take ownership of your content. It's important to own your own content. This is vital. Anyone with any integrity will support this. As always with life, you need to read the fine print and only deal with someone who lets you keep ownership of your own content.

For those of you who are curious, there is a tool inside Traffic Geyser that lets you upload Podcasts. We also have tools inside Instant Customer that allow you to upload media files. All of these tools can be used in Podcasting. End of not-so-subtle commercial ;-)

The last step is to update the RSS feed. The RSS feed is what broadcasts to the world that there is a new episode available. In most cases, the RSS feed update will be automatic based on the Podcasting system you are using. In other cases, it is a very quick update. Never write this yourself – this is the kind of thing they invented computers for.

That is it! That is how you make and publish a Podcast.

Summary

Making and publishing a Podcast is a simple process. The three steps are: creating a media file, uploading the media file and updating the RSS feed.

When creating the media file, it is best to use a method that you are familiar with or get cheap and easy direction on how to do it.

Secondly, upload the media file. This is even faster and easier than creating the file. Just be sure that you use a system that supports this. Also, read the fine print and make sure you are with a host that doesn't take ownership of your content.

Lastly, you will need to update the RSS feed accordingly. In most cases this will be automatic, but in the event it is not, it is a quick process.

Action Items

1. Create the audio, video or text-based media file. This should be fast, quick, easy, and based on what you know.

2. Upload the media file to a hosting site that supports Podcasting and allows you to keep ownership of your content.

3. Update the RSS feed if your service isn't automatic. Forget that, go with a service that makes this automatic.

4. Make sure you send your receipt for this book to **Bonuses@PodcastStrategiesBook.com** to get a list of our recommended services.

QUESTION SEVEN

What is the fastest way to make a Podcast?

When many of us think of Podcasting, we have an image of a $6,000 an hour recording studio with snobby engineers and headphones and wires everywhere. This studio of course, was reserved sixth months previously at great expense and tapping into all the connections you have. Oh, the pressure. Fear not, part of the power of Podcasting is you need a lot less tech and need none of the drama described above.

The two fastest ways to make a Podcast are to "call it in" or hire it out.

"Calling in" a Podcast in is simple. The way this works is you have a microphone; connected to a computer; and you simply "call-in" your content, leaving an audio file when you're done. Think of it like you're leaving a voice mail message – something you'd "call in." With this process a 5-minute Podcast takes, get this, 5 minutes.

How cool is that? How low pressure is that?

Yes, in many ways, "calling it in" is synonymous with "recording it yourself" but the imagery and ease of calling something in is the same relaxed approach we want you to take in producing your Podcast. It should be as simple and as natural as leaving a voice mail message.

Once you have your content, you can always add intro music, edit out any coughs, and save as an .mp3 file for your Podcast—it's that easy.

The same Audacity program we recommend for editing will let you record a Podcast episode directly to your computer (part of why we recommended it.) The price for that one is still free, so spend your money on a microphone.

In addition, there are several apps for your Smart Phone that will let you record an audio file. Many of them are a dollar or two and produce great results. There are many high-end microphones designed to make your Smart Phone sound like the recording studio described above. Want something really easy?   Both Traffic Geyser and Instant Customer have options for using your phone to literarily call in a media file – and the phone doesn't even have to be "smart" at all.

We are big believers in "fast." However, if you have to record a file so that it comes out sounding really good, use a good USB microphone and the Audacity software. You can also apply an audio filter called a compressor and audio exciter to make it sound better. This will yield a high quality, basically free, audio file perfect for Podcast.

It is important to point out that although, yes, you can "call a Podcast in," it is important to remember the age-old truth that you "never get a second chance to make a first impression." The content of your Podcast will always be more important than how it is delivered - but if they won't listen (because of the audio) or watch (because of the video), you have done yourself (and your audience) a tremendous disservice.

When you send in the your receipt for this book (**Bonuses@PodcastStrategiesBook.com**), we'll get your information on great microphones and video cameras than can be grabbed at a surprisingly low price. There are many options available for under a $100 and we recommend you do what you can to sound and look as good as you can.

Another option is to hire out the Podcast recording. There are people who will come to your office and set up the recording for you. This allows you to just show up and focus on creating the content. If you hire out the recording process, once again, make sure that you read the fine print and that you own your content when you are done. This process can be surprisingly inexpensive as well.

Summary

Calling-in or hiring-out your recordings are the two fastest ways to make a Podcast. It doesn't need to be complicated at all.

Calling-in simply requires that you call-in your content and leave an audio recording using a smart phone or a computer.

Another option is to hire out the Podcast recording to a third party. In this instance, they set up and record the Podcast for you, leaving only the content development to you. If you end up using an outside resource, just be careful that you're dealing with an ethical organization and that they allow you to retain ownership of your content.

Action Items

1. For speed, call-in or hire-out the recording of your Podcast.

2. If you need a high quality recording, use a good microphone and recording software on your computer – or smart phone. Also, consider applying audio filters to make your recording sound better.

45

3. If you want to just focus on the development and delivery of your content, hire-out the recording process to a third party. Just be careful that you retain all rights to your Podcast.

QUESTION EIGHT

What is the best Podcasting software?

The rule of thumb for using Podcasting software is, "What you know is always better than what you don't know." What this means is, if you know GarageBand, use it. If you know Audacity, use it. If there is an obscure piece of audio editing software that you learned in college and it gets the job done, great, use it! The best Podcasting software is the one that lets you create content quickly and easily. We also want to strengthen the point that there is nothing wrong with hiring it out if that puts you at ease.

Podcasting is about content – not the tech that makes the content possible.

When recording audio, we are big fans of Audacity because it works on both the PC and the Mac – and makes editing your Podcast easy. It's not as complicated – or as feature rich as some of the other programs out there, but it is more than any traditional Podcaster will need.

If you own a Mac computer, GarageBand is wonderful software and it's free. If you're familiar with the program, you already know that it is very easy to operate. If you aren't familiar with it, you can visit your local Apple store or search YouTube for tutorials.

If you have a PC, Sound Forge by Sony is under $100 or Sony Movie Studio (formally Sony Vegas) is a really great option. If you are going to do what they call "movie studio" for video on your PC, Sony Movie Studio (formally Sony Vegas) is the best product out there.

The RSS creation should happen in conjunction with your publishing. Select a web-based Podcasting program that automatically takes care of the RSS feed when the media is uploaded. Many people go through this process in conjunction with their blogs and it is often automatic.

Lastly, make sure you have a media hosting system that gives you statistics about your shows and information about your audience. You want to know what episodes were popular so that you know how to direct your content in the future. We've seen some Podcasts where Episode X gets 200,000 downloads and Episode Y gets 80 and Episode Z gets five. What is the difference? If you don't know the difference between how episodes were received, you won't know what works or what doesn't.

Summary

Hands-down, the best Podcasting software is going to be the one that you know. If you don't have one that you are already familiar with, Audacity is a great option.

When selecting a web-based hosting platform, choose one that automatically takes care of the RSS feed when the file uploads. Many Blog platforms do this – as do almost all Podcast hosting providers.

Make sure you track what episodes are popular and which aren't is also important. Without this knowledge you'll be unable to tailor your content to your audience – *or know how incredible you are.*

Lastly, just remember, there is nothing wrong with hiring the process out if you want a smooth, stress-free experience so that you can focus on your content. We do believe this is why you got into this game originally.

Action Items

1. If possible, use audio/video editing and/or Podcasting software that you are familiar with. "What you know is what's best!"

2. Audacity and Cross-platform are great options for both Macs and PCs.

3. If you own a Mac and want to use free Podcasting software, use the *GarageBand* program that comes with your computer. If you have a PC, you can use either Sound Forge by Sony or Sony Movie Studio (formally Sony Vegas).

4. Choose a Podcast hosting platform that supports automatic RSS creation and updates.

5. Lastly, use a Podcasting software system that tracks activity so that you can take advantage of its "what works and what doesn't" insight.

QUESTION NINE

Where do I host my Podcast?

So you want to find a Podcast hosting provider? Google or Bing (or whatever your preferred search engine is) will work for your search. Check reviews and you'll do fine. A copy of your receipt for this book sent to **Bonuses@PodcastStrategiesBook.com** will let you know our favorites at any give time. Because things change so quickly, we don't want to put something in print that we don't have the ability to retract.

Be careful of people promising that which they cannot deliver! A Web host and a Podcast host are not the same thing. As a result of thumb, traditional Web hosts with "unlimited bandwidth" do not have Podcasting compatibility because of the possible runaway bandwidth costs that could happen if an episode went viral.

Your service provider will pay attention to what files are coming off of your host. If it notices audio and video files in large volume, they will know you are probably hosting Podcasts and, unless you have an explicit agreement that says you can, they will most likely shut you down. This means people who are trying to download your content won't be able to and they will likely end up mad and potentially ignore your outreach of content in the future.

You never get a second chance to make a first impression.

Of course, the worst part of this is that it's not going to happen at 2:00 A.M. when nobody is downloading. It's going to happen when something significant is happening: you go viral; iTunes is now listing you as a featured Podcast; or somehow you were mentioned somewhere else and a whole bunch of people are trying to access your content. This is not the time when you want to be shut down!

That's why it's imperative to make sure you have a host that provides Podcast compatibility. Ask them if they have an "up time" promise and know what it is. This is the key to on-demand content delivery.

Finally, there are a couple of Podcast hosting providers who, if you read deep enough into their fine print, think that they own your content. This is morally bankrupt, a silly idea and bad strategy – but other than that, we're all for this approach.

Summary

You should look for a few key things in a Podcast hosting provider. First, make sure that they have Podcasting capability. Regular search engines like Google and Bing may suffice for your search. Do take note that many hosts with unlimited bandwidth don't extend this to Podcasting.

Ask your potential host if they have an "up time" promise that explicitly allows for Podcasting. If you don't, you are liable to get shut down during a Podcast that could result in alienating your audience. You don't need to stand for that – there are plenty of options.

Make sure that you own your content with your host.

Action Items

1. Select a host that has Podcast capability. Regular search engines like Google and Bing work great for your research, just be clear on their hosting limitations.

2. Use a service provider that explicitly outlines their "up time" promise and that you are permitted to Podcast. This is the key to on-demand content delivery.

3. Don't be silly enough to work with any provider who claims ownership of your content.

QUESTION TEN

How do I upload my Podcast?

So, you have a Podcast episode? You've created media ready for the world? How do you upload it? Is iTunes involved? The good news is that it's painstakingly easy. In fact, it's probably one of the easiest parts in the Podcasting process.

Most Podcasting systems, on the Mac or PC, will let you go to a Website page and upload it from any desktop. Some will require an FTP program. However, you will find plenty of FTP programs out there and available for your use.

Some apps automatically upload your Podcast. Our favorite is Bossjock Studio. With Bossjock, you can record your Podcast right on your iPhone or iPad and instantly publish it to your publishing place. More apps and options are listed in our online gear guide.

Again, you always have the ability to hire any part of this process out. If you already have someone creating and editing your Podcast for you, you may want to have him or her do the uploading for you as well.

By the way, you don't have to worry about iTunes in the media uploading process. More on that in a future chapter.

Yes, we have easy upload of media content at both Traffic Geyser and Instant Customer.

Summary

As you will see, uploading your Podcast is an extremely easy process. Ninety-nine times out of a 100, it's a Web-based process where you can upload your Podcast directly from your computer or the app you're using to create your Podcast.

In a few occasions you may need an FTP program, but the good news is that there are many FTP programs available and most of them are free.

One of our favorite methods is to upload using the Bossjock Studio App that allows you to record your Podcast on your Apple device and upload directly.

If you find any part of this challenging, you can always consider hiring it out.

Action Items

1. Upload your Podcast directly from your computer through a simple, web-based program.

2. Use the Bossjock Studio App to record your Podcast on your iPhone or iPad and then directly upload and publish.

3. Hire out this part of the Podcast process if you prefer to remain focused on the Podcast content and not the process.

QUESTION ELEVEN

How do people get updated when I release a new episode of my Podcast?

This is one of the most misunderstood elements of Podcasting. It's also part of what makes Podcasts so exciting. There is a misconception that there are numerous distribution channels that you have to alert every time you record and release a new episode. However, this is the magic of Podcasting—you don't!

Podcasting is set-it-and-forget-it.

Instead, the way it works is you submit your Podcast to the right directories, once, when you first released your Podcast to the world. Then, when you update your RSS feed, they automatically notify everyone on your behalf.

How do you tell people when you have released a new episode of your Podcast? You just have to release a new episode of your Podcast!

We recently published a new episode of one of our

Podcasts. Before it was even posted to our website (we took a coffee break), we checked the stats and there were already seven downloads. People who were subscribing to the Podcast were so excited to get the next thing.

Can you imagine an audience that is tracking your new content that closely?

This is part of the beauty of RSS and the entire Podcast system. You only have to submit it once and then the Podcatchers go to work, automatically checking for updates.

Now, this does not mean that you don't have to market your Podcast. Unfortunately, many people think that that marketing of a Podcast is also a "set it and forget it" type of situation. I mean, iTunes does the marketing for you, right?

In reality, your audience is only going to have a Podcatcher that checks for a new episode if they have subscribed. It is your job to get them to subscribe.

In order to get your content widely distributed you still have to do all the work you would do with traditional marketing. You always want to have "new blood" and new customers. Just realize that the "old blood," for lack of a better term, is covered by this automatic update.

Yes, Podcasting is that cool.

Summary

When you add a new episode to your Podcast, your Podcasting system should update your RSS feed accordingly (and automatically). After you update your RSS feed it (automatically) notifies all of your subscribers that a new episode is available. This is all accomplished just by releasing a new episode!

It's important to remember that you still have to conduct your normal marketing efforts in order to keep "new blood" flowing into your customer base.

Action Items

1. Tell your subscribers that you have released a new episode of your Podcast just by uploading and releasing the new episode. When you update your RSS feed it automatically notifies your existing subscribers.

2. When it comes to advertising, however, don't "set it and forget it." Continue with your traditional mode of advertising to ensure you keep attracting new listeners.

QUESTION TWELVE

How often should I Podcast?

The most important part of Podcasting is maintaining a consistent relationship with your audience. Podcasting has the power to inspire people to consistently seek you and your content out on a regular basis. Once your audience has said "hey, I'd like content from you on a regular basis," you might want to consider delivering it.

Ask yourself the following question: If there is someone you want content from, do you want to know it is coming every Tuesday or do you want to know it is coming whenever they feel like releasing it? Think about that, if you know it's coming every Tuesday, you can start to predict it. Once you become predictable to your audience, you become part of their lives. This is intimacy that marketers could only once dream of.

There are people who have even called Podcasters saying, "Hey, I expected to listen to you on my drive into work this morning. Where is the latest episode?" Now, that is an audience that will buy from you and invest in the services and systems you have to offer. That is an audience that wants YOU.

The key is to be predictable and consistent. Consider your audience. Are they the type that will listen to a daily Podcast? If so, give them a daily Podcast! I'm not saying you should create a Podcast every single day: create a batch of Podcasts once a week and then have them distributed accordingly. Computers are great at automating that kind of thing.

The flip side to all of this is that you have to be aware that your audience is busy—everyone is. Whatever you do, do not waste their time. Do not do anything that would make them ask, "Why am I listening to this?" Be consistent, but don't waste their time.

Strive to consistently release Podcasts weekly or biweekly. You may even stretch this to every three weeks if you are delivering video Podcasts. This will depend on the content you are releasing and will be determined on a case-by-case basis. There is some content that you may not want to have released every week.

One of my favorite bands waited almost three years between album releases. Wondering what was taking them so long, I thought they were being lazy. Then all of a sudden I heard track one play, "I don't want to waste your time with music you don't need." Beautiful.

One thing we do recommend is, even if you are consistently delivering a new episode every Tuesday morning at 8:00 A.M., give people a chance to be notified when a new episode comes out. Not everyone uses a fancy Podcasting program that notifies them of updates! And if they do, they aren't always paying attention to them.

Releasing new Podcasts provides you with a great chance to interact with your audience. If you can, capture their phone numbers and emails so you can text them or email them whenever a new episode comes out. There is something that is very powerful and popular about being contacted about the release of new content.

Be consistent and be predictable, but do not in any way overwhelm your audience.

Think like a show producer. By providing a specific date and time people will start to think about it like the subscription that it is.

The great thing about traditional broadcast media, which encompasses radio and television, is that everyone gets conditioned into thinking they have to show up for a channel or show at a specific time. Similarly, the more you schedule your Podcast releases, the more of an imprint it leaves with people versus being loosey-goosey. People will respect and trust you more by having some level of discipline and rigidity. This is an exceptionally important aspect of creating a sustainable, long-term audience and brand.

Summary

The frequency that you should release new Podcasts revolves around maintaining a consistent relationship with your audience.

How often you release new episodes will rely, in part, on your audience's preferences. However, weekly, bi-weekly and even every three weeks intervals have proven to be effective. Remember to be consistent but not bothersome. Give people a chance to receive notification of your update.

Start thinking of Podcasting like producing a show, and pretty soon you'll have your audience anticipating the release of your new episodes just like they anticipate their favorite radio and T.V. shows.

Action Items

1. Use Podcasting to maintain a consistent relationship with your audience and build rapport.

2. Depending on your audience and your content, release new episodes weekly, bi-weekly, or even every three weeks.

3. Use the release of your updates as an opportunity to capture contact information so that you can communicate future releases and news to them directly.

QUESTION THIRTEEN

Is it possible to do paid/premium Podcasting? Is that a smart move?

Can you charge people for your Podcasts? The simple answer is yes. However, it's important to realize that right now almost all Podcasts are free. For many people the term "Podcast" means free. The average person, surrounded with a myriad of Podcast choices, is psychologically going to have a hard time buying a Podcast when they can get so many of them for free.

That said, we have seen this shift toward paid content in television and there is no reason to believe it isn't coming to the Podcast space. In the 60s and 70s it was completely foreign to even think of paying for television. Today, it is completely foreign to actually know that you don't have to pay for television! Similarly, the Podcast industry is bound to change. However, at the time of writing this book, the majority of Podcasts are free – and we think they will stay that way for a while.

There are services and tools that will let you create and

distribute paid content (including via Podcast). It's not a smart move by itself, but there are some models that have worked as part of a bigger project or bigger member site. One that comes to mind is Dave Ramsey, the financial radio host. He has a membership system and inside of the membership system that holds his software, forums and tutorials, has provided members the ability to get all of his shows commercial free as a Podcast. Dave is making a killing doing that.

Charging for content is not necessarily a bad idea. You just want to make it part of a larger platform or system. It's that whole "Integrated" model of Podcast monetization we examined earlier.

The key here is to immerse yourself and see/match what others are doing. See what the big names and brands are doing and model them. One model to consider is a comedian named Dan Klass. Dan had a free Podcast called *The Bitterest Pill* for the longest time. It was free and it was even delivered without commercials. At one point he took highlights from *The Bitterest Pill* and made them available as CDs inside of iTunes. People were actually paying .99 cents a track to get a Podcast they were already getting for free. At one point Dan was offering a Premium Podcast but at the time this was written he took that option down.

You can still get Dan's CDs on iTunes. By the way, they're hilarious.

So, is it possible to do paid / premium Podcasts? Yes, it is. Is it a smart move? …That is the deeper question, at least at this time and place in the industry.

Summary

In short, yes, you can charge people for your Podcasts. However, the larger question is whether it is a smart move considering that most Podcast content, at the time this book was written, is being distributed for free.

Charging for content is not, in itself, a bad idea. If you choose to take this route we encourage you do some thorough research into other models that may be working and consider making your paid Podcasts part of a larger member site, product or system.

Action Items

1. Examine other paid content models in the industry. Immerse yourself and see what other big names and brands are doing and potentially model them.

2. Consider your audience—are they rabid fans, clamoring for your content? If so, perhaps there is a larger model that could draw in revenue. Also considering bundling your paid content with a bigger offering.

QUESTION FOURTEEN

How can I get my Podcast to rank high in iTunes?

Let's start with one simple fact: iTunes—like Google, Coke, and Kentucky Fried Chicken—has a secret formula. However, the formula for rating high in iTunes has not been released. That said, we can certainly move forward and deal with what we know.

And we do know a lot.

We have taken over a dozen Podcasts to top ten status in their particular category. Every time we set out to do this we have ranked high in the top ten. Many of them have even been rated number one. We actually had a student who beat out Oprah Winfrey for about four hours. That was enough for him! *If you beat Oprah for four hours, that is a press release you must get out there.*

Based on what we know, the way to rate high in iTunes is to obtain a lot of subscriptions in a short period of time. Our educated guess to explaining and understanding iTunes rankings is that to rank high, 80 percent of your score is based on how many subscribers you have had in the last twenty-four hours. Again, this isn't an "official" number as there is no such beast – but we seen it closer to accurate than anything else.

There is a very simple way to accomplish climbing up the iTunes list. Take your list and make it highly beneficial for everybody to subscribe to your Podcast at a specific time.

If you go to iTunes right now and you look at all the top Podcasts, you'll notice that most of them have something in common. Most of them are radio shows, television shows or movies. Is it because radio, television, and movies have the most viewers? No, it's not. We've seen the numbers. Why are they ranking as the top Podcasts?

If you analyze the list, there are several Podcasts that are getting two, three, or four times as many downloads who aren't in the top 10. Why? It's simple. NPR's *This American Life*, Dave Ramsay and Jim Cramer—at the end of every single episode they get the chance to say, "Subscribe to my Podcast." Apple in turn sees these new people subscribing to the Podcast on a regular basis and that keeps them at the top of their game.

What can we learn from this? Never stop asking people to subscribe to your Podcast. You simply want to tell people to subscribe to your Podcast through a regular and consistent process. In order to build a regular subscriber stream, make this part of your educational process.

Place "Subscribe to my Podcast" in every email and every piece of social media or marketing collateral. Make it part of your complete and total marketing mix. Realize that it's bigger than your Podcast. Realize that people know, like and trust you when you have a Podcast.

Why do people listen to three hours of Dave Ramsey and then go subscribe to his Podcast? It's because they know, like and trust him. You want to create the same thing. Once you start getting people to subscribe to your Podcast, it's no different than any other media platform out there.

So, how do you get to the top? It takes a lot of subscribers in a very short amount of time. In order to break into the Top 10 list on iTunes you need, on average, 200-300 subscribers over the course of two to three hours. Although the initial rise is doable, the only way to stay on the charts is through gaining a regular stream of subscribers within iTunes through ongoing marketing efforts.

Remember, this is ultimately about engagement. When you're asking questions, when your audience feels involved with you and you're constantly telling them what to do, you will improve your number of subscriptions – which will put you higher up the charts in iTunes.

What about reviews inside of iTunes? We can't tell if they have a direct impact on your iTunes positioning, but let's face it, if someone is looking at your Podcast, and there are a lot of reviews, you've got a much better chance that they'll subscribe.

Summary

Even though the secret formula for iTunes hasn't been released, we've figured out that the way to rate high in iTunes is to obtain a lot of subscribers in a short period of time. From what we can tell, 80 percent of your score is based on how many subscribers you receive within the last hour.

The simple way to climb up the iTunes list is to take your list and make it highly beneficial for everybody to subscribe to your Podcast at a certain time.

It's important to never stop asking people to subscribe to your Podcast. Just tell people to subscribe to your Podcast through a regular and consistent process. One way to do this is to simply tell people, "Subscribe to my Podcast" on every piece of social media and marketing collateral you produce.

People get to know, like and trust you through your Podcast. When your audience feels engaged and involved, you're bound to improve your number of subscriptions and ultimately climb higher on the iTunes ladder.

Action Items

1. In order to rate higher in iTunes, your ultimate goal is to obtain as many subscriptions as possible in a short period of time. You can do this by taking your list and making it highly beneficial for them to subscribe to your Podcast is a short window of time.

2. Never stop asking people to subscribe to your Podcast. Place "Subscribe to my Podcast" on every single social media and marketing collateral piece that you produce.

QUESTION FIFTEEN

How can my Podcast stand out against all other Podcasts?

Getting your Podcast to stand out against all other Podcasts, in the end, comes down to the fundamentals of marketing.

The first thing you want to create for your Podcast is your album art. Seriously, do this before you even record your first episode. Think about your favorite CD or album art. Do you have that image in your head? Well, that's exactly what you want to create for a Podcast—gorgeous album art. If you have a million-dollar Podcast with a nickel piece of Podcast art, your audience isn't going to click the subscribe button. Quite frankly, they're not going to be interested. The great part is, there are a lot of graphic artists and designers who will create that piece for you ridiculously cheap.

You also need to create engaging descriptions, content, and keywords for your Podcast. This gets down to basic SEO. Use the terms that your audience is likely to search for. If you never pop up in your audience's search inside of iTunes (or anywhere else), they will never have the opportunity to know you exist, let alone subscribe.

You also want to have as many reviews as possible in iTunes. Think about it. If you go to YouTube, and look up a video and the video only has one view, you know that one view must be that person's Mom or significant other! People get excited and are attracted to Podcast profiles – heck anything - that have a bunch of reviews and five-star ratings. You'd be surprised how few people pay attention to this.

As an exercise, go to iTunes and type in the topic of your choice. You'll see how few Podcasts there are with attractive album art and good descriptions, with just a couple of reviews. I keep saying this, but...*you never get a second chance to give a first impression*.

Let's be honest here: When your audience looks at your album art, description and reviews, they're going to make their decision without every listening to your content. Good art and reviews will get them to click subscribe.

You also want to populate your listing with reviews from listeners. You can gather these by saying inside your Podcast, "If you like what you heard, please go to iTunes and give me a good review." You'd be surprised how effective this is. If you really "spoke" to someone in your Podcast, they might be very willing to give you a good review, just like they might pass along a funny email or share a viral YouTube video.

At the same time, you'll also want to elicit reviews externally – outside of iTunes and the Podcast directories. Inbound links tied to your Podcast will bring your rankings up inside of Google. You don't just want somebody saying inside of iTunes, "This person is great." You want someone inside of Facebook and Twitter saying, "This person is great."

Here's an effective little hack I borrowed from Mike Stelzner at *Social Media Examiner*. Take a look at **http://www.PaulColligan.com/love**. If you click on that, it takes you to a page that automatically pre-populates a tweet on Twitter that supports the Podcast. If anyone in my audience loves the show all they have to do is, with a click of a button, tweet to all of their friends that love. All I have to do on the Podcast is say something like … "If you loved this Podcast, please visit http://www.PaulColligan.com/love. You'd be surprised how effect that is.

Podcasting and social media go very powerfully together. iTunes has direct Share to Twitter and Facebook – use that / mention that / direct people to that. As a matter of practice, every time you do a new episode, share your new episode immediately through both social media platforms and you'll do great.

Summary

Just by doing these three simple things: creating great album art, writing great descriptions and practicing systemic marketing for internal and external reviews, your Podcast will stand out against all the other Podcasts. Throw in some great content once they subscribed and you're well on your way past the others.

First, your album art can make or break your audience's first impression of your Podcast. A million dollar Podcast deserves million-dollar artwork. Thank goodness it doesn't have to cost that much.

Second, write Podcast descriptions that not only accurately represent what you are offering to your audience, but are also designed to bring you some traffic from the search engines.

Lastly, don't neglect your marketing efforts to gather internal and external reviews, as these are what will really set you above other Podcast listings.

Action Items

1. Create compelling album art to visually influence your audience to subscribe to your Podcast.

2. Develop well thought out descriptions, peppered with keywords, to draw your audience to your

Podcast in search (iTunes and otherwise).

3. Put in place a strategic marketing approach for gathering internal and external reviews. Don't be afraid to ask for support of your Podcast.

QUESTION SIXTEEN

How do I get listeners for my Podcast?

Getting listeners (*and even more listeners*) starts with an entry in the iTunes directory, but it's not the entire process. It's actually a lot like the Google directory – you certainly want to start there – but it is never the whole picture.

Getting inside the iTunes directory is simple. After logging into the iTunes store, click on the "Podcasts" button in the upper navigation bar. When you arrive on the Podcast page you will see "Podcast Quick Links." Click the "Submit Your Podcast" button. It's that's easy. It's real; it's super simple and absolutely free.

Note: We're not including a screenshot here because iTunes always changes their interface – but the location and process hasn't changed since day one. Follow the directions above, regardless of your version of iTunes, and you'll be able to submit your Podcast to Apple.

Realize that the majority of people who look for Podcasts

inside of iTunes are in fact Podcasters themselves. The average person is generally not going in to iTunes to find Podcasts related to their interests – *they're just not that into Podcasts yet*. Yes, your Podcast will change that for them, eventually, but they probably didn't start looking for you in iTunes.

Do, please, take all the steps mentioned in the previous chapter. They're essential – but not the entirety of your strategy.

Many Podcast audiences (like all audiences) are built by word of mouth, sometimes through social media and perhaps by the occasional search. Acquiring new listeners for your show is as much about being found outside of iTunes as it is being found inside of it.

Another important realization is that most of your audience simply isn't *looking* for a Podcast and most of your listeners certainly aren't *listening* for a Podcast. Rather, they're listening for *content* that you're making *available* by Podcast. I hope you understand the difference.

In short, if you dominate iTunes, you're only going to dominate the world of Podcasters. In reality, you want to dominate a much bigger realm than that.

It's about connecting with your audience through every level of communication. Every single vehicle of communication is out there at your disposal, so make it easy to subscribe. Put subscribe buttons everywhere! Offer Click-To-Subscribe links in the footers of your emails, on your Website and in your social media.

Here's a trick to make subscribing easier. In order to subscribe to the *Ask Paul Colligan* Podcast: go to http://www.AskPaulColligan.com. If you were to type that link in right now, it would automatically redirect you to the iTunes subscribe button. Now if someone asks, "How do I subscribe to *Ask Paul Colligan*?" You can tell them, "Visit AskPaulColligan.com." It's nice, simple and super easy. Audiences like easy. Easy is always good.

Lastly, visit StitcherRadio.com and set up an account there to make your Podcast available on that platform. They're doing some interesting things in the world of on-demand media that you'll certainly want to be part of. The great thing is SticherRadio.com will also give you great stats.

So, that's how you get listeners for your Podcast.

Summary

An effective strategy for getting listeners for your Podcast starts with uploading your Podcast to the iTunes directory so that it can be found by anyone looking for it; however, it requires greater outreach than that. Isolating your efforts to iTunes may help you dominate the world of

Podcasters, however, it's your additional marketing efforts that will enable you to dominate a much larger sphere that includes your listeners...and their friends...and their friends of friends.

By focusing on creating amazing *content* that is merely *distributed* via Podcast, you will realize a much larger reach, outside of iTunes.

Make a concerted effort to reach out to your audience through every means of communication available to you. Placing "subscribe" buttons in every piece of marketing collateral—emails, websites, and social media—will dramatically expand your reach and organic word of mouth.

Action Items

1. Make sure you Podcast is submitted to the iTunes directory as the first step in getting listeners for your Podcast.

2. Expand your marketing reach beyond the world of Podcasters by including "subscribe" buttons on every form of collateral available to you. Imbed buttons in your emails, website and social media to name a few.

3. Make subscribing easy for your audience by creating a simple link to immediately redirect people to your iTunes subscription button.

4. Lastly, gain further reach by setting up an account with SticherRadio.com and making sure your Podcast is available on that platform.

QUESTION SEVENTEEN

How do I assess if my target audience is a good match for Podcasting?

I know a lot of people are saying, "This all sounds great Paul, but I don't think my audience and customers who buy my products and services would even subscribe to my Podcast. Why should I do this if I don't think it's going to work?"

The simplest way to find out if your audience is receptive to Podcasting is to ask them. Nice, simple, easy. The answer might really surprise you.

Now, don't ask them outright if they listen to Podcasts, because that's not the point. The point is to ask them something along the lines of, "If I made free content readily available to your phone, your computer or your television, is that something you'd be interested in receiving on a regular basis?"

They'll say yes if they *know, like* and *trust* you.

People want benefits – not solutions. Don't sell them the drill. Sell them the hole. What kind of benefits is your audience looking for? You're delivering that via Podcast. Don't worry about the "how", because the "how" is free and easy. People will use Podcasts if they get the benefits they want in the first place.

Think about it. Can you conjure up a single person out there who has content that you want and is offering to make it readily available to you, quickly, easily and simply for free? Why would you say no?

For example, if my bookkeeper said to me, "Paul, I've got a Podcast. You should listen to it," I'd be so freaking bored out of my mind that I would never click the subscribe button. However, if he said, ""Paul, I'd like to send a five-minute tax tip to your phone every Monday." I'd like that. Fifty-two things I can do to lower my tax bill! How is this useful content going to be sent? It just happens to be a Podcast.

See the difference? It is subtle - but huge.

The sub-question in this is: what if I don't have an audience? What if I don't know them yet? What if I'm using this to build and position myself, which we chatted about earlier?

The simple thing to do is to go into iTunes and see if there are any Podcasts about that topic. If there are, now you know that your audience is listening to Podcasts. If there aren't any, that doesn't necessarily mean that they're not interested in Podcasts. That just means that no one has filled that niche yet. At this point, go into Google and search that term. If you search the term and there's content about it, then you might seriously want to consider Podcasting about that topic. Again, it isn't about the audience, it is about the content the audience is looking for. Why wouldn't they want you to provide them content at the time, place and device of their choice?

Your true audience will always welcome specialized content and the benefits and results it delivers.

If your audience doesn't want your content, then in reality, they're not your audience.

Remember, at its core, Podcasting is not about the technology. Podcasting is not about the iPhone or Android or audio versus video. Podcast is not about RSS feeds and .mp3 files. Podcasting is about creating and delivering content quickly and easily – in a way your audience is ready for, and hungry to consume.

Summary

The simplest way to find out if your audience is receptive to Podcasting is to ask them. Ask them, if you made free content readily available to their phone, computer, or television, would they be interested in receiving it on a regular basis. Their answer will tell you tremendous things about your audience.

People want benefits – not shows. What benefits is your target audience looking for? Tailor your Podcast to the delivery of this content. Make it available to them in a quick, easy and simple way.

How do you know if there is an audience for what you want to Podcast? Dive into iTunes to see if there are any existing Podcasts on the subject. If there are, you know there is an interest level in the content. If not, this may be an indicator of an untapped market!

It's important to remember, your true audience will *always* want to consume specialized content that confers benefits and positive results. Anyone else is quite simply, not your audience.

Action Items

1. Ask your audience if they are interested in receiving free content, made readily available to the technology of their choice, on a regular basis.

2. Take a moment to consider what benefits your target audience would be interested in. What are they looking for? Deliver this content via Podcast.

3. Go into iTunes and search for the content terms for what you want to deliver. If you find that Podcasts already cover the subject, you now know that there is an audience. If you don't find Podcasts on topic, this may mean that you have discovered an untapped market...time to strategize!

QUESTION EIGHTEEN

Who owns the copyright for a Podcast? Can I use copyrighted content in my Podcast?

This is a classic question - one that we get all the time. We'll start by saying **we're not attorneys and we're not giving you legal advice** (we don't even play ones in a Podcast). We're just sharing what we know here and what has worked for us in the past.

First of all, the fundamental element of copyright law is that you own what you produce, the second you produce the content. Point blank, you own the copyright for the *content*. It is yours. The law protects that.

As a result, who owns the copyright for the Podcast? The answer here is *the people who produce it.*

Some unscrupulous Podcast hosts will try and take ownership. They basically make you sign on the dotted line saying, "If you host with us, we own it."

Don't agree to this! It's silly. *Read the fine print.* Make sure that someone else doesn't take ownership of the content that you've created.

(Again, we're not lawyers and we are not giving legal advice.)

In the terms of using copyrighted content in your Podcast, here's the deal: it's a bad move. Using someone else's copyrighted content on your Podcast is an easy way to get into trouble. Just don't do it. Forget what you've heard about "fair use" or anything else.

And, really this is your chance to shine. Don't use the content of others – use your content. This is what your audience is there for.

What do you do about the music and content you want to add to your Podcast? It's simple: search the Internet for royalty-free images and music that specify they are usable in a Podcast medium. Make sure that you have the rights to put the content in your Podcast and you are good to go.

Summary

As long as you created it, you own the copyright for your Podcast. Makes sense, if you think about it.

Some Podcast hosts will say they do. Don't sign a contract that silly.

Make your life easier by not using copyrighted content in your Podcast. If you must, make sure it is royalty free content that says you have the right to use it in your Podcast.

Action Items

1. Exhale; you own the copyright to Podcast content you produce, as long as it doesn't contain the copyrighted content of anyone else.

2. Double check that your Podcast host doesn't think they own your content.

3. Avoid using copyrighted material in your Podcast that's not yours. If you must, use royalty free music that specifically allows use in a Podcast.

QUESTION NINETEEN

How can I make my audio sound as good as possible?

So, they've signed up for your Podcast. They've downloaded an episode. They just placed some expensive ear buds in their ears and they click play. How are you going to sound?

How can you make your audio Podcasts sound as good as possible? Use the best microphone you can, positioned well with as much background noise eliminated as is possible.

If you don't already have a high quality microphone, you'll want to get the best one for your money. This doesn't mean you have to spend $1,000 or more. This literally means to go out and get the best microphone that you can. No more, no less. If you send a copy of your receipt for this book to **Bonuses@PodcastStrategiesBook.com**, we'll get you access to our online Gear Guide that not only suggests and recommends our favorite stuff (at any given time), but also shows you were to get it for the cheapest price we could find.

Positioning

Once you have your microphone you want to position yourself, physically, so that you are as close to it as is possible. Why do you want to get close to the microphone? Because the closer you get to it, the less noise it will hear that isn't you. Think about it – it just makes sense.

Remember all those music videos you've seen of recording artists in the studio singing their hearts out an inch or two away from the microphone? This isn't a dramatic effect to make the music video look more impressive; it's what they know – because it brings the best sound.

If you are having challenges with getting too close to the microphone, to the point you hear spitting noises, you'll want to get what is known as a "pop filter." You can buy these for $20 or $30. Honestly, don't let your neighbor see this, but you can actually take a wire hanger, wrap it in a circle, put pantyhose over it and you've got yourself a home made pop filter. It's not that complicated. Look up "Handmade Pop Filter" on Google and you'll do fine.

If you do record video of yourself on your microphone and are using a homemade pop filter from some old panty hose, we can't guarantee the results there.

Background Noise

Children and pets in the background can be quite noisy and distracting. To take care of this, duct tape your children and your pets to a closet wall and you'll have no problem at all.

Just joking!

Not really.

Yes we are.

Do what you can to eliminate background noise. Silence your phone, shut your doors and windows and let the children know that you're recording.

Here's a hack back from the days of the BBC War Correspondent. How can you record good audio when bombs are going off or there is shooting going on around you? The fact of the matter is BBC Correspondents of old would put blankets over their heads and talk really close to the microphone. The hack still works to this day and I've recorded hours of content with a blanket over my head. Some say I should record video content with a blanket over my head, but that is another topic all together.

Often when you're listening to an amateur record audio,

you can hear a lot of what's called "room ring." That's just an echo from talking inside of an empty room. To help with this you can stack pillows behind your microphone to stop the reverberating and bouncing off the wall noise. You can also hang carpets, tapestries and acoustic foam on your walls or ceiling to buffer the noise. Acoustic foam is a great strategy and very inexpensive. You can look it up on Amazon.

Although there are various hacks available to make your Podcast sound as good as possible, a good microphone, close to you, with a pop filter is literally 95 percent of the process. I've seen people who have spent $2,000 soundproofing their room before they ever bought their first microphone. Think about this intelligently. Think about it strategically. And you'll be fine.

Remember to send your receipt for this book to **Bonuses@PodcastStrategiesBook.com** so you can get access to our online Gear Guide (we'll keep it constantly updated with the latest gear (and make sure our interns track down the best prices).

Some of the audio recording programs (including the free Audacity) have noise removal features that you might want to examine. Removing noise after the recording is as much of an art as it is anything else. Note: *always* check the final results when you have the computer remove noise, as you might not both agree on what is noise and what is actually content …

This probably goes without saying, but this is another point where you might want to consider hiring out the engineering of your audio.

Summary

Using a good quality microphone with a filter that you talk into closely will get you 98 percent of the way towards making your Podcast sound as good as possible. Remember to use the best microphone possible. You can find many great quality microphones for under $100.

Be as diligent as you can to block out background noise. This does not mean duct taping up the children, however, turn off phones, close the doors and windows and remove as much surrounding noise from your environment as possible.

Action Items

1. Get the best microphone possible for your budget and outfit it with a pop filter. You can find many quality microphones on Amazon for under a $100. Don't want to buy a filter? Check the Internet for DIY instructions and make your own!

2. Position yourself as close to the microphone as possible when recording audio to get the best sound.

3. Remove as much background noise as feasible. There are many options to accomplish this that range from stacking pillows behind your microphone to holding a blanket over your head.

4. If you've done the best you can to make your Podcast recording sound as good as possible, but you still have disruptive sound in the background of your recording, consider using software to help you remove more.

QUESTION TWENTY

How do I record a Podcast if the participants are in two different physical locations?

O.k., now we're getting fancy. Not satisfied with a long drawn out monologue? Want someone else to mix it up with you? Have you found that they're not in the same physical location as you?

Does having guests (or co-hosts) on your Podcast in a different city make for some exciting possibilities? Of course it does. Pulling it off is much easier than you might expect.

There are three options for recording a Podcast if you're in two different locations.

The first is Skype. At the time of the writing of this book, Skype does not have recording capabilities built into it (yes, really and yes, we agree silly) so you'll need a Skype recording program.

Audio Hijack Pro is a great program for use with Macs. Another one is called "Call Recorder" from the Ecamm. It records decent audio and video, does side-by-side video and costs less than $20. On the PC side, you can use a program called Pamela for Skype. It works pretty well and only costs around $20 too. Again, send us your receipt for this book to **Bonuses@PodcastStrategiesBook.com** and as new options for recording Skype come up, we'll let you know.

One thing that a lot of people don't realize about Skype is that you can use it to call regular phones (landline and cell) as well. For example, if you want to do a phone interview with someone, like on a radio show, you just need a Skype account along with a few dollars of Skype credit to place the call. At the time of writing, calling a phone from Skype was just a few pennies per minute ala cart, and less than $3 a month for unlimited access.

One of the cool effects of this process is that your voice will sound like you are in a radio studio as a result of being on a good quality microphone, while the person you are interviewing on the other end, on the phone line, will sound a little tinny. It's that fun radio effect that we're all familiar with. Use it to your advantage.

In my experience, Skype has always been a great idea – but it is often a great **idea**. The real world implementation of Skype in an interview is never perfect (drops happen all the time, the program can crash, voices go away, the wackiness of the Internet kicks in, etc.) and this fact needs to be acknowledged in the development of your Podcast Strategies. If you have the prefect guest for your show, do you really want to subject them to the finicky nature of Skype?

One last point on Skype is that Microsoft recently purchased them. Historically, Microsoft doesn't have the best track record when it comes to improving technologies that purchased. Again, buyers beware!

The next option is a Digital Hybrid that is used for audio recordings over the phone. Basically, what happens is it takes a phone line and it processes and mixes it in a way that makes for the best possible sound for recording. Then it lets you talk into a quality microphone while you are in turn talking to someone who is on the phone. It's what all the radio stations use for their call-in shows. You know the sound – the Digital Hybrid is the tech that makes it happen.

The last option is a bit techie, but we're going to share it anyway: it's called the "mix-minus." In simple terms, what happens is person A records on a good microphone at their location, while person B records on a good microphone at their location. Later, during post-production, you edit the two audio recordings together in the studio.

How is this final mix accomplished? You usually take a

third recording of just the phone and then line everything up based on what you see on the phone. The last step is to take out the phone piece, after which you end up with a great quality recording.

Once you get the hang of this technique, you'll find that it produces great audio and requires very little tech. I once got an email from someone who told me to "stop lying" and admit that my co-host and I were in the same room when we recorded our Podcasts. I take that as a high compliment.

Side note: there are cheap audio editors out there for hire who would be more than willing to mix together a mix-minus recording for a very reasonable price. Again, your job is the content – not the tech behind it.

Summary

There are three options for recording a Podcast in two different physical locations: Skype, digital hybrid and mix-minus.

Skype is a simple and easy solution to record an interview through computers or even to call a landline directly.

Take the digital hybrid route if you have the cash and want to wire it up yourself.

Finally, you can use mix-minus if you want to go ultra-cheap (and effective).

No matter what mode of recording you use, stay focused on your main outcome—getting your content out.

Action Items

1. Don't worry about recording a Podcast with a co-host or guest that isn't in the location as you. You have plenty of choice.

2. Use Skype if you are seeking an affordable, easy and simple means of connecting Podcasters located in two different locations. Get an inexpensive third-party call recorder and you are set. Do know that Skype can be finicky and strategize/plan accordingly.

3. The digital hybrid route is another option for recording audio if you want to do the easiest possible phone interviews. You'll sound great and the person on the other end will sound as good as is possible.

4. Use the mix-minus technique if you want to get a bit more technical and have a good microphone at your disposal at each physical location.

QUESTION TWENTY-ONE

Are Podcasts good for my topic? What if my topic is very visual?

There are three questions to ask yourself: Does your audience care about your topic? Does your audience want content, or, as we stressed earlier, the benefits of the content? Does your audience ever find themselves **not** in front of a computer screen?

This might come as a surprise to you, but people in the visual arts get into their cars to drive to work or go for a run or bike ride to get some exercise. Although they are largely anchored to visuals and computer screens in their job, they are not completely tethered to it. If your audience actually cares about your topic and wants the benefits of your content then it is OK if you don't have visual representation in your Podcast.

What's great is it becomes a means by which you can bring them into something else and touch them in an additional way. While everyone else is hitting their eyeballs, you can connect with them in a place that nobody else is.

Still unsure? Realize that your Podcast can be recorded, transcribed and then converted into an e-book, Kindle Book, PDF, ePub or put into another visual medium for those who need it. There have actually been Podcasts where people record the audio and then hire graphic designers to create visuals to compliment the audio file.

Yes, again, we're back to that "integrated" strategy of Podcast monetization we discussed earlier.

Finally, are Podcasts good for your topic?

As we mentioned before, if your audience cares about the topic, benefits and results you offer, then yes, Podcasts are an effective tool.

Always remember, although audio is currently the 800-pound gorilla, it's not your only Podcasting option. There are numerous other mediums out there.

Summary

When considering if Podcasting is good for your topic or if it works with a visual-based audience, ask yourself the following three questions:

Does your audience care about your topic?

Does your audience want content or the benefits of the content?

Does your audience ever find themselves **not** in front of a computer screen?

If you can answer yes to these then Podcasting can be an effective tool for your topic.

Action Items

1. If your topic has an audience and that audience would like to consume content not attached to their computer, you might have a match.

2. A traditionally visual topic can certainly be presented as an audio Podcast. It opens up doors to that audience that your competition isn't using yet.

3. Still need visuals? Take your Podcast and have it transcribed. Use the transcript to create other mediums of content like an e-book, Kindle Book, PDF, or ePub.

Gear, Etc.

A Few Thoughts About Gear

Because the world of Podcast gear and software is always changing, we're not going to place our entire gear chapter here. Anything we say, any price we mention will probably be moot by the time you get this book. As a result, we've put the entire Guide online and will be updating it on a regular basis. Merely send a copy of your receipt for this book to Bonuses@PodcastStrategiesBook.com and we'll make sure you get a copy (and access to the updates).

Here is the kind of content that Guide contains:

Both audio and video Podcasting involve a number of tools for production. While it may seem overwhelming at first, there are actually only a few components that you will need to start creating Podcasts. Lets start on the Audio Podcast side, since all the tools used for audio will also be useful for video Podcasts as well.

No matter what your level of commitment, or your budget, you will need the same basic items to record an audio Podcast. These are a Microphone, Headphones, and a computer with audio editing Software. The computer acts as the hub for the microphone recording your voice as well as any sound effects you may want to play. It also provides an audio monitor sound for your headphones so that you can verify that the sound being recorded is at the level you want. Finally the Audio Editing Software can be used to change the recording after it is made, allowing you to clean up problem areas where the sound is too quiet, too loud, or where outside noises can be heard, all prior to making the Podcast available online.

For Video Podcast we would add a Camera of some type as well as Video Editing Software. A video camera should allow you to preview the shot in a viewfinder, or on a computer display, so that you can be sure that you are only filming what you intend. Being able to preview the shot will minimize the number of retakes. Video editing software will allow cutting and splicing of recorded video to either remove uninteresting portions, rearrange shots into a better series, or to clean up any unintended images before releasing the video Podcast.

While the cost of doing a video and audio Podcast may be as cheap as the cost of your smartphone, there is much functionality gained when additional and more specialized equipment is added to the mix. Podcast equipment setups can be broken down into three general categories - Basic, High Quality, and Professional

Quality. Keeping in mind the list of necessary equipment, we can look at each category and pick equipment that best fits the desired results and budget!

The most basic Podcasting can be done with an iPhone. For audio Podcasts, plugging a quality headset with a microphone, like a apple earbuds or Bose AE2i and using an audio recording app such as RODE Rec will allow you to create a recording while previewing what it sounds like on your iPhone. Adding a Rode iXY microphone or SmartLav microphone would further improve the sound quality. Both GarageBand and RODE Rec have noise gate filters that reduce background noise if you are not recording in a quiet environment.

After finishing recording editing can be done right on an iPhone or iPad in GarageBand or for more options audio should be copied to a computer (Mac or PC) and then edited with Audacity - a free multi-platform audio editing program.

For Video Podcasts, the iPhone can also be used as a video camera. One thing to keep in mind is that the front camera, which is on the same side as the screen, is not as good a quality as the back camera. So, although it is possible to use the front camera to record yourself, the quality of video will not be as good. For better results you can get an iPhone case that mounts on a tripod.

While there is not much video control with an iPhone, it

will do a decent job of video quality provided you have good lighting. This means that you should not be outside with harsh sunlight, or in front of a bright window. Instead you should be in a controlled light environment where most of the light is coming from in front and above you. For high quality and professional levels we will talk about using studio lighting, but for a basic setup it simply a matter of making sure that the light source is not too harsh, that you don't have shadows in the image, and that the background is not distracting.

For a Podcast with a bit more time and budget, there are some improvements to equipment that will result in Higher Quality of both Audio and Video.

For starters, a dedicated Microphone should be used. There are 2 main types of microphones available - Condenser and Dynamic. The main differences are sound sensitivity and price. Condenser microphones range from $125-2000 and require power (generally referred to as phantom power) to operate. They are more sensitive, so you can be a bit further away from the microphone and still get sound good. The other type is Dynamic microphones, which range from $20-500 and do not require power. These microphones are less sensitive and so require more boosting and need to be physically closer to the person. The advantage of this type of microphone is that they tend to work better in noisy environments, as long as the microphone is close to the speaker. For a good sounding microphone plan on spending $100-250.

To get the audio from a microphone to a computer you will need either a mixer/audio interface or the microphone needs to have a USB connection such as the Rode Podcaster Dynamic Vocal Microphone. Many manufacturers now make USB versions of their microphones in the $75-300 price range. Using a USB microphone does add some simplicity since you are able to plug the microphone into any USB port on the computer, but generally USB microphones have minimal options for control beyond sound level.

A better approach may be to use a mixer with an audio interface such as Behringer Xenyx Q802USB USB Audio Mixer. This will allow you to have one or more microphones, as well as other audio devices like iPods, to be plugged into the mixer and then a single mixed audio stream would go to the computer for recording. A mixer allows you to adjust the loudness, and often to change the sound characteristics like equalization of the microphone. It also provides the phantom power that condenser microphones need. Lastly, the mixer is useful when you are combining several sounds sources for playing jingles, sound clips, or including a Skype conversation on a Podcast.

Headphones are very important because what you hear in the headphones will direct how you adjust the sound of the Podcast. If what you hear in headphones is not accurate, you may be adjusting the audio of the Podcast in a way that will make it sound worse for others.

Headphones, which you may like for music, pumped up bass and lower mid-tones are not what you want for editing a Podcast. The best headphones for editing will have a very flat response - meaning they will reproduce the audio as closely to how it was recorded as possible without boosting bass or any other frequencies. A good headset that is used by many Podcasters is Senheiser HD 280 Pro. This headset is mid priced at $125 and is a very good value for the money.

Software is a matter of preference, with many high quality Podcasts being created using the same free Audacity software recommended for a basic setup. To add some functionality in processing the Podcast recording you can use Apple MainStage software, which can either add digital processing and effects to a live audio signal, or be used by itself to record a Podcast start to finish. You may also want to use a Soundboard app if your Podcast will include lots of clips or jingles to simplify the playing of them. Finally, while it is a more advanced topic, you may want to stream your Podcast live while you are recording it. In this case Nicecast can be used to both record the Podcast and to stream it live.

For Video Podcasts, you will want a nice multi camera setup. You could do a video Podcast with a single camera, but it is much more interesting for the viewers to see a 2 of 3 camera shoot. Even with just a single person talking on a Podcast a two-camera shoot allows you to change the angle of the shot without having to move the camera by cutting back and forth between 2 cameras. On larger Podcasts, or when several people are involved a three-camera shoot will bring an almost professional look and feel to the Podcast. If the budget is tight and a good quality single camera shoot is all you need, a good pro-summer DSLR like a Canon 60D, will produce great video with sharp focus and a fuzzy background. If going for a multi camera shoot, it is certainly cheaper to go with multiple digital 1080p camcorders. The image won't quite be as dramatic as a DSLR, but for the cost of a single DSLR with lens, you could pick up 3 of the JVC GZ-EX310 camcorders.

For the rest of the Guide – with the latest prices and options, *send a copy of your receipt for this book to* ***Bonuses@PodcastStrategiesBook.com***.

Now What?

Your content deserves to be consumed anywhere possible, on any device possible, and you now know how Podcasting can help make that happen.

As mentioned in the beginning of the book, we want to keep in communication with you. When you send your receipt to **Bonuses@PodcastStrategiesBook.com**, not only will we send you the bonus package listed, but also there are a few other things coming your way that will help tremendously.

Please send in your receipt now so we can help you on your journey ahead.

And, … If you aren't in front of your email, call us or text us at (503) 928-6740 with your name and email address and we'll make sure to get that info to you.

It's that good ;-)

See you (hear you) in iTunes, and everywhere else.

Paul

Made in the USA
Charleston, SC
15 May 2013